THINGS WE CANNOT KNOW

THINGS
WE CANNOT KNOW

ALAN GERSON

MBF PRESS
Montgomery

MBF Press
105 South Court Street
Montgomery, AL 36104

Library of Congress Cataloging-in-Publication Data
ISBN-13: 978-0-9785311-6-4
ISBN-10: 0-9785311-6-7

Design by Brian Seidman
Printed in the United States of America

www.mbfpress.com
www.newsouthbooks.com

*This book is dedicated to my wife Beth
and in memory of my parents*

Contents

Introduction

Patricia Roger

I first read these poems by Alan Gerson in the fall of 2005, in Ponchatoula, Louisiana, where I had evacuated to escape from Hurricane Katrina. I stayed in Ponchatoula for seven and a half weeks, waiting to return to New Orleans. During that time, our original group of three people, three cats, and a dog was joined by my husband and son, and our good friends Alan and his wife Beth, whose evacuation began near Lafayette. I've known Alan since 1986, but I never knew he wrote poetry. We met when he began law school at Tulane University (not in law school, but in the cafeteria, where we and a group of law and graduate students in English ate lunch together regularly). I quickly became a fan of his paintings, which are visually beautiful, intellectually interesting, funny, and often moving. We had some time on our hands in Ponchatoula and one day the conversation must have turned to poetry and Alan let me read these poems. My favorite poems are the more visual ones, some of which show an artist's eye, such as "Baroque Volute," "St. Peter in Chains," and "Girl on Vespa," yet I also value the more philosophical poems and have learned a few things from them, for example, what a Saros cycle is (a period of 6,585.3 days used to predict eclipses of the moon and sun) and what the Goldbach Conjecture is (every number greater than two is the sum of two prime numbers).

About half of the poems in this collection are abstract and philosophical meditations on subjects such as faith and uncertainty, and half use vivid visual images often to capture a moment—a young girl twirling on the beach at sunset in "Grayton Beach"—and convey the feeling that moment inspires. Of the visual poems, a number are haiku: "Cat Dreams," fifteen haiku (with fifteen syllables each, "except for one," instead of the usual seventeen) that capture some of the characteristic movements and postures of cats, and "The Sound." A trip to Italy inspired most of the other visual poems.

The poems reflect Alan's education and career. He is the youngest son of parents active in the Jewish community in New Orleans and he majored in philosophy at Boston University. Poems such as "I Am a Terrible Jew," "Belief Is Desire," and "Faith's Mechanism" show a struggle between faith and doubt. "The Antimonies," "Das Denken Ist Schwer (Thinking Is Hard)," and "Stumbling into Exile" focus on ontological and epistemological questions. The more visual poems, I think, are connected to his experiences as a visual artist. After graduating from college, Alan returned to New Orleans and began his career as an artist, receiving an MFA from the University of New Orleans in 1980, making prints and painting, as well as serving as the Visual Arts Director of the Contemporary Arts Center in New Orleans. After graduating from law school and working as an attorney for a few years, Alan returned to art full time. Some poems, for example, "Girl on Vespa," can be visualized almost like a painting: the green, red, and white of a girl on a Vespa speeding by, her long leg and frowning face captured in bright acrylics. "Baroque Volute" presents a more complicated canvas of the interior of a church or cathedral in which the stained glass, painted ceiling, wooden trim and pews are in motion: "carved circles whirl," "whorls of deep sienna/Crash over rivers of oak/And baroque volutes cascade through mahogany currents," while "Pink bottomed cherubs/And fat laughing nymphs/Float in great flowering heaven."

The idea that we must live with uncertainty is emphasized in both philosophical and visual poems. For example, "The Antinomies," a poem in four parts, balances an awareness of the fact that we cannot know much for sure with our desire for some certainty. The first part, which focuses on what we know, ends with the speaker affirming, "More information/Will not lead/To certainty." The second part seems to define existence (but not definitely). It focuses on a "time-like interval" that the speaker characterizes by what it is not—"Not a flow . . . Not a being," and finally calls this "interval" a "task," and later "the act of intending," "the fact of a life." The third part considers history: the speaker says that though "all nows are different/In the world's unfolding;/ . . . all that has passed/Is necessary/Now." He indicates that we choose to believe that what happens is inevitable, that when we think we are using "pure reason," we are still subjective. In the last part the speaker focuses on "the moment." He advises living "in the constant storm/ Of unpredictable history/And with the frantic energy/Of emptiness." In "The Fortress Orzini," a poem that illustrates uncertainty visually, the speaker claims that Sorano, the town where the fortress is located, is "falling," "crumbling," "melting"; the ravine beneath waits for the town to fall into it "with jaws wide open," but he says that he and his companions look and smile: "Sunflowers grew tall near Sorano/And uncertain soil held us aloft—/We smiled at the world that danced around us."

"Po, Not Edgar," another poem set in Italy, also illustrates the theme of uncertainty in a traveler's feeling that a place which cannot be familiar is somehow familiar—the phrase "oddly familiar" is repeated in each stanza. The first stanza also recalls for me some of Alan's childlike paintings: "Oddly familiar/This flattening/These poplar trees/The blue flames—/A child's drawing." The second stanza presents "Moats but not castles," and "farms but no farmers/In Dolo Mirano," and in the last stanza, the image of a valley is interpreted as "a slow acquiescence/To the water's lapping." The speaker sees this image as acceptance of "the dissolution/On which we live," a "balance," he says, "And oddly familiar/In a foreign land."

Other poems tell stories. "The King's Penis" tells of an encounter of travelers on a bus with "a little man with something wrong." And some are joyful and exuberant, like "I See the City." The first stanza even rhymes: "Open the door/And fly into the light/ I see the city/Shimmering beyond the night." "Main Highway" celebrates life as well. The speaker "speaks of" the pleasures of a weekend with friends: crepes, raspberry preserves, lemon curd with scones, chocolate tort, shortbread and tea (one friend is a baker), stars, rain, a toolbox, "Japanese plums framed in the window," "red rubber boots and porcelain cups." He "speaks of" singing and dancing; "That long night was full with us."

The poems in this collection ponder *Things We Cannot Know* and seem to suggest that while we are pondering, we can also take delight in experience.

Things We Cannot Know

The Antinomies

I
Our list of God's integers
Depends on what we know;
But
It is accepted
That no set
Of measurements
Is ever complete:
More information
Will not lead
To certainty.

II
A time-like interval—
Not a flow;
But a being.
Not a being;
But a task—
Obscured
By nothing.
It is the act
Of intending.
It is the fact
Of a life—
Mystical
Or generalized away.

I say it is not superfluous—
Saying what cannot
Be said.

III
All nows are different
In the world's unfolding;
But all that has passed
Is necessary
Now;
Through the choice
Of inevitability
And the application
Of pure reason
We snag the artifacts
Of subjectivity
And learn the methods
Of coincidence.

IV
But
For the moment
We'll overlook the implications
And dream of something
That cannot exist;
And separate what is
From what happens
Because
You must be sure
Of your decision's
Uncertainty
And be willing

To live
In the constant storm
Of unpredictable history
And with the frantic energy
Of emptiness.

TRANSIENT IMPRESSIONS

Acid subtlety
Informed piety
A lancet of fact
And the cauterizing wit.
A momentary frisson,
The ambiguous knife
And then the complex blessing
Of the particular language.
Decretum horrible—
The terrible potential
Of every implement—
Disarticulation
And blindness.
But these are just
The discursive preliminaries
"Laudandum, Ornandum, Tullendum."

BENEATH THE CIMABUE

What I cried
For then is what
I cry for now.
For I have
Never learned
The wisdom of fish;
And while
She taps her shoe
Beneath the Cimabue
Lovers
Iridescent
Coalesce
And fade: huddled
In a dark arrow
Beneath the Dome

THIS ROOM

Transparent with desperation,
Long shadows lie on Zimple Street.
He tries to explain
The interior uncertainty—
His tangled development.
"There is a solution somewhere"
But the point now fleshed
And organized
Is choked on sentiment;
Circumscribed
By his son's bad dream.
Though his intuitions were sound,
He would not admit
That there was not
A rhinoceros
In this room.

OUR PRESENT ANOMALY

The monkey in the mirror
Tapping at his finger:
Such woeful knowledge.
The idea of reference;
Dreaming
Nature's quantum dream.
Predicting,
At random
Those chance events;
And by gambling,
In the context
of a systematic world
Explaining
Our present anomaly.

FAITH'S MECHANISM

There is only one lesson
And everyone learns it:
To choose,
In a mechanical universe.
Every proposition
A subject with a predicate—
Reason constructing
Experience
By faith's mechanism.
Everything may be explained
And mean nothing.
The end
Must be unattainable—
Its realization
A certain possibility.
Because in us
Is not always of us,
We may have knowledge of things
We cannot know.
To see the thing
Is to give it a context—
The source of orientation
A resonant pattern.
It is the context of belief;
The proven unknowable.

7, 8, 9

He carries the *I-Ching* everywhere;
Listening to the wood complain,
The floor vibrating like an instrument
As plump sissies pirouette
On tiny feet
And leap.
"Noverim me, Noverim te"
He prays on his knees; hidden
Within the resined mist of the Paraclete;
Circumscribed by his son's bad dream—
Redefining the notion of purity
And tracing the cause of his woe
To the conjunction of moments
And the dangerous optimism
Of some distant purpose.
He concedes
There may be a certain utility
To the rules of consequence,
Though certainty
Is not the same as necessity.
He is his own end
Resisting nature's conclusions;
If only he knew the soul's
Relationship to space.

Das Denken Ist Schwer

(Thinking Is Hard)

I

"The world," he said,
"Is the totality of facts."
There is no hidden meaning;
But there is a response—
Of sorts.
A language
That can be agreed upon,
Maybe.
Transmuted elements, Weakly interacting particles,
The curve of probability,
And a promise of compromise;
But for us the world
Is too fast to see.

II

An incomplete symbol;
Beyond being;
The perfect emptiness.
Indefinable.
A correspondence
Between nothing
And everything
And one thing.

Qualities In Objects

A troubling presence,
Plausible in the abstract
But so diminished by calculation
that even, with their delicate avoidance,
The saints cannot escape it.
Outside that question there is no response,
And though necessity determines
its own falsehood the problem
Remains constant.
Researching the wide range of particulars—
It is established
That refined answers and remote consequences
Are not signs nor indications
Nor evidence
Of established norms.

A slight fissure
Allows the diffuse faith of shadows
To expand and resonate and fill
The plump world we know,
If only for a moment:
But an uncertain transition
To the inevitable doctrinal imperatives
And comprehensive syntax
Leaves an uneasy juxtaposition
Of folly and turbulence.

Yet, this crystal life presupposes
Geometric degeneration: the paradox
laid bare
Through voluptuous criticism
And transient impression.

Tempering irreconcilables,
We are seduced by abstraction
And the conjunction
Of beautiful objects.
Yet there remains the problem
Of proof within the old framework—
Where truth grows with time
And generates
A world composed of incompatible parts.
That infinite moment, though hidden,
Is ignored at one's peril.
There can be no movement
Without acceleration:
Dies Irae, Dies Illa
Solvet Saeclum in Favilla.

A BETTER GOD

A better God answers
Our insatiable expectations
With a metaphor of convenience,
And the enchantment of statistics.
A question is posed—
In the fullness of that wave
And of all those waves
And in the sterile science
Of pretty systems:
The mind
Of an observer observes
The underlying calculus, poised
Between the danger
Of consistency and the beauty
Of complete answers;
And takes note
Of this prudential algebra—
So useful to travelers
In this, our congenial wilderness.

THE AGREED FRAMEWORK

Staring into the middle,
An intersection
Of diverging observations.
Black energy—
And a tail of silk
Circles, evergreen,
Now that the angry summer
Has passed.
Fish flying deep
Sense the value of obscurity—
Measuring a thing
That cannot exist.
But while a certain form
Of energy is unfolding
The search for sequence
And understanding continues;
Using the language of logic,
And amplifying the effect
Of that bewildering instrument,
They begin another calculus
And press its shape to the limit.

BELIEF IS DESIRE

Belief is desire.
Hidden congruencies
Aching—impossible
To imagine.
Memory's density
Diluted by whispers,
Transmuted truths,
And the sinister
Influence
Of objectivity.
Laden
With significance
And the uncertainty
Of judgment—
In ambiguous circumstance
We posit
An analogy of structure;
And decry
The coruscating effect
Of multiplicity.
Predicates, though neglected,
Still search for subjects:
Finding relics
Of incomplete symbols
And impressions
Of complex objects

Arisen but bereft
Of context; and floating
On the currents
Of a hypothetical future.

BRIEF NEW WORLD

The thought's soul
Full of intimate confusion—
Ripe for rationalization,
Contemplating
The odd poignancy of an object.
A spate of conjecture
Full of necessary imaginings—
Announcing the restoration
Of siegeworks lain;
And instructions revised.
Now a provocative gesture
Full of recursive horror—
Regression buried in the light
Echoing the holy re-revelation
Of uncertain night.
"Di mi se mai fan tutti alcuna cosa"
full of unfettered reasoning—
and pregnant assertions.
The void, too, is a form
Of multiplication.

EXOUSIA

Fleshly reason's discourse,
Full of calculated compassion
And moral statistics—whispers—
Wisdom is an economy of truth.
The tympany is thumped
With varied emphasis
And attendant angels,
Hands outstretched, sing
With charmed duplicity.
The eye of prophetic illusion,
Wary of perspective,
And hard with windy melancholy
Is propelled, even floating, 'til
Abruptly it too
Dissolves in a map of water,
Weeping—
"But the word must have a context.
There is a world and not
Nothing."

I Am a Terrible Jew

I

I am a terrible Jew
And betting (literally)
That, if He is above,
The lord will forgive me.

II

The aesthetic of reason—
The wisdom to fit in.
I divide the indivisible;
And scribble in a lapidary style.

III

But I see now
That it is grander
And darker than ever
I might have imagined.

EXEMPLUM

Rooting for palliatives
In the structure of taste—
Lappets and leaves are lifted
And cover the minatory flesh
Hidden in the naked gesture.
But again we concern ourselves
With the danger of metaphor;
And those conflicting conceptions
Buried in a single image—
Their vague remit to serve
Only the clarified disillusion
Of this, our brave new logic;
Diffused and unmethodical
They remain unresolved
While the internal contradiction,
Safely implanted, continues speaking
In the language of blind revelation
And with desperation's well reasoned desire.

SOFT AUGURY

The variant aims
Of a difficult situation—
Detached resistance
And a contingent truth
Held at bay.
Vague passages lost,
Proving the proposition false
But not improper;
And with the ruthless intuition
Of many-bellied melancholy
The hard allusion
And bitter sentiments
Glide one into the other:
A catalogue of incidents,
The torrid conjecture,
A cushion of assumptions,
The soft augury
Maundering—
A prophet in the bog
Sinking but not yet lost.

Stumbling into Exile

Stumbling into exile
Settling in
To the routine
Of endless criticism.
Reiterating again
The improbable notions
And the doctrines
Of a long dead conflict;
And in other contexts
The thought
Once seriously thought
but now
Dissected, and rendered,
And made harmless—
Nearly.
I answer the charge
Of incompleteness
With beautiful ambivalence:
Things indifferent
Things immutable
And for them
A terrific purpose
Denoted
By the external word
Found in the floating world
Of tantalizing restriction
And inchoate possibility.

AMLETH

You will be
And then
You won't be:
But for me
Wisteria
Is the problem.
Torches are lit
In winter's
Twilight blue,
And there we
Note
The poignancy
Of a father's gift
When disappointment
Flits
Across the face
of his son,
But the scene survives
The actors' intercession
As they read
From their index
Of small demands.

BIX

All of life's lessons
Were misconstrued
But he listened
For improbable evidence
Of the hidden
Context.
Laying the horn
Against
His chest
(gorget
of vivid instants)
he spies
the object of his dream, now
writ on large bits
of manuscript;
Trumpeting
Symmetry's conundrum—
the difference
Between the river
And its current.
By random genesis
Dark angels will
carry his desire away.

Theory of Aspect

Abstract notions
And practical devices:
Dual desires
Accepted without demur.
The narrow space
Persists
Between description
And endless
Reiteration.
Indifference
To any premise
Must remain
For the sake of uniformity
While rival patterns
And anonymous
Messengers fade
In the long night
Of many days.

Pale Eye

I
Clover conceals
Conflict
In the settling
Countryside.
Green battlefield—
Silent abattoir.

II
That
pale eye
Follows me
Through black
Thatch;
And
Cold night's
Bright
Crossing's
Patched
White here
And there
Beneath.

THE SOUND

White line—
Brief scar in the sky.
Ice on thorns.
The sound
of wood and water.

DEATH BY DISTANCE

Death in the shallows,
Where the dispersed fraction
Cant upward
To clouds of men
And the eternal recession
Of unfurled colors.
In the blue distance
Grey rivers rise;
And fluid victory hardens,
Concealing
The significance
Of distant water
And the disadvantage
Of loving association.
Atrocious rain pours torrents
Of fitful information—
Congealing facts bob
While spavined prophets,
Limp with fear, fret;
And peering
Through the stark prism
Abandon irretrievable
Decisions to others,
Even less deserving.

WANSEE

We contemplate
The actionable language
Of hoary sin;
And rejecting
The central metaphor, fly
With a bad conscience
From one critique to another.
Having knowledge enough
To presuppose—
The mordant count begins.
Lists without mercy lie
In line awaiting crisis,
Still pregnant
With contradiction;
And finding a different content
We create clearer motives—
The better to reach
Our inevitable progress.
Bearing the revelation
Of an insistent template
We see a dimmer vision
Of frightening conscience
And the vicious empathy
Of gloried self-interest.

THE SAROS CYCLE

I

Brief illumination.
The probabilities
In a heap of stones.
Dark lights and pieces.
Rumbling, murmurous tales
Of variant fortune
And children lost at sea—
Their apparent forgiveness
Also drowned
In that debatable land.

II

Now guilty of imagining—
While learning to do wrong
And seeing the advantages
Of murder
When everyman doubts
the other.
With the new law lost
Deep in his breast,
Surprised by the old realities
And exquisite subtleties
Of this immediate dilemma,
He seeks a tactical surrender
While the fatal cravings
Of lesser men

Are obscured
By the mystery of battle.

III
The shock of sameness
Amid foreign designs
And the chance survival
Of a silent creature
Spitting shadow beams—
Bats among birds fly,
And orbit a cooling sun.

IV
Ordinarily,
There are other choices;
But distracted
By another enthusiasm,
Seduced by loyalty,
And recognizing the danger
Of gratitude
The hunger
For evidence persists
While the inevitable
Moment of inertia
And the fires of supposition
Leave lying obstacles
Of ash, rock and dust—
And the vague outlines
Of an ancient landscape
Disappearing
In the reddening twilight.

GRAYTON BEACH

Sand on her thigh
And nearly floating
Julia is spinning.
Her towel is white
And full in the wind.
At the edge of red night
The curled lip of water
Reaches her feet
Where Julia is dancing
Another arabesque;
And the ocean's breath,
Now risen, is visible
In her hair combered,
And born by the wind.

THE FLAT EARTH

The flat earth
Blue below heaven;
And
The dark remedy
Beneath me,
Lying,
Coiled in the belly.
We see
The frenzied peace
Of the tree-lined street,
As continents
Sway in the breeze;
And while many worlds
Travel their courses
The cocks crow
And black beetles click
Along on hard
Brittle feet.

DISTILLATE

A bed
Full with grim reward.
Its past remains clear
In form, soft
And soiled—
Limned in white.
Sullen jokes
And a bit
of jagged light.

Death Leading a Pagan

Stelae provide no
Satisfactory answers:
Nor Seth, falcon headed.
A sculpted wall carries
The shadows of acrobats;
And even in rain the lady
In her landscape cannot
Say what she wants

A Nice Question

Acidic letters,
Anger fed.
Built brick upon brick
Thundering
Insistent impotence;
Pounding
At the unguarded gates.
Painful conference
Of debtor
And creditor
Seeking
The balanced vacillation
Of blame
And agitation.
Cold breath,
Faint in the chamber,
Softly intoning
A tactful compromise;
But cheerful betrayal
Is the end
Of all our plans.

THE GOLDBACH CONJECTURE

I can't tell the story
But I know
There is truth in what they say.
The habit of association
And moral measurement
Have led to a code
That nervous clerics
With all their instruments
Pitter-pattering in black robes
Won't break;
And broken symmetry's now
All that's left in the end.

HEAVY-SET MAN IN STRIPED SHIRT OR CARNIVAL SUICIDE

The big picture
Of open geometrics
And the laden table
Covered by creased trousers.
A marble fountain
Of bachelor's wives
Etched in glass
Waltzing with the spoon girl
And her mallic-molds
Brooding in the fluid tree.
Arbitrary measuring stick
Whipping large tragic heads.
He takes his fundamental breath
Before *le petit mort* flies
To that figure in the dark landscape;
And coincidental dogs (or blood
Machines) fill the metronomic
Bucket with winged figures.
Long forgotten horizon
Of an azure day pulls
The uncertain dreamer
Deep underwater to a red
Cavern where pencils on a plinth
Recite the Celebes couplet.
But for her spatial wedding

Worldly wisdom should be painted
On wood. Though the present
Piece, she says, is all that matters.

THE DIPLOMAT

In retrospect
Doom should
Have been foretold
But now there is no
Use in recalling
What might have been.

The implication
Was plain to see
For those who would;
But contrary winds
And a barren show
Of power obscured
Deliberation.

Lavish promises
And ambivalent
Demonstrations gained
Time, but only just.
Ambiguity
And circumlocution
Left thistle, dust
And desolation.

And indirect observation
Confirmed that vision

As an accurate description,
But seen at a distance;
And already reflecting
An impression of the idea
Of a thought of the action.

External objects
And the resentment
Of injuries may be
Infallible, but not
Always so; and occasionally
Lead to the illusion
That a sound argument provides—

Though inferences
From afar belie
The perception
That things will always
Appear as they are.
Those faint images we see
With references beyond us
And in the bright
Sunlight still are hidden
From these, our persistent
Selves; peculiar objects
That die forever
Without being born.

The observed phenomenon
Of constancy or
An uncertain compliment
Provides coherence

And a framework for
The resultant fiction
That the relationship
Between events

Heralds. Intentions
Best construed
As the source
Or our factual belief
That the constant
Conjunction of instants
Will add up
To more than a sum.

Resentments Reconsidered

A species of danger
Was clearly in mind;
And appropriate action
Was haring its way
Through the disordered contest—
Forecasting triumph,
Portending menace.

Hypothetical conspiracies
Crafted by the crises
Of contemptuous prophets
And artificial aristocrats.
They hold the detested
Instrument up and shout:

"We are not as we once were!"

Committees of apostasy,
Frantic with paralysis
And darkened by influence,
Prefigure the interpretation
That lay behind the choices
Made in such elaborate confusion.

The ensuing dynamic
Of croaking choruses
And oscillating salients
Was scarcely affected
By the silent operation
Of the document
And all that went with it.

And though the premise
Was unclear the logic
Grew ripe for exploitation.
An abhorrent extension
Of the dear argument
And the calculation
Closely reasoned.

Pelf and agreements unuttered,
Boodle grasped in parentheses of action.
The moribund resurrection
Of the leader without followers—
Yet with loyalty orotund,
Fecund and spawning dread:

"Where is the sword then, if we compromise?"

Corrosive orthodoxies, desiccated specie
And resentments reconsidered.
We find redemption in the reflected passion
And virulent friendship
Of privileged monsters.
But now, we think, the apparatus is degraded
In its new form.

We follow a harsh fugitive running
From nettlesome abstractions shouting:

"We must abandon their notions, their logic."

Recalculation in this context—
Now freedom swallowed by quiet
Division and disconcerted
Reality. Events contingent
And chronological; strange
Elements and ominous evidence;
Nothing ahead but discord and deviltry.

Preserving the fiction
With ad hominem restraints
And a patina of plausibility
The names mean nothing now;
They point to nothing now
And the old issues are gone;
Lost, finally, in the liquefying
Embrace of disillusion.

Cat Dreams

15 Haiku — each 15 syllables except for 1

1.
Pale sky
White cat.
Blue shade
Bamboo
Shivering.
Grey dusk
And night.

2.
Cat dreams
Tapping rain
Black bird on branch
Wet leaves
Barely green.

3.
Shadow blade
Cutting
White wings
In silent vine.
Thorn pierced sky.

4.
Uncurled tail
Pointing.
Cat in basket.
Boundless moment.
Clouds passing.

5.
Yam-bodied
Mother of many
Listens.
The highway hissing.

6.
One follows
Another
To the field.
Not hunger.
The quick kill.

7.
Toy on string—
Three-legged cat
Blue jay shrieking.
Foot on table.

8.
The garden.
Two cats.
Empty cage.
Eyes in the dark.
Broken bowl.

9.
Noise.
Cats stop.
White Bottle.
Heads are turning.
The man is poring.

10.
Light wedged
On stairs.
Black window.
Cat poured
From chair.
The smell of grass.

11.
Amber cat
On map of branches
Walks
Through sun
Cracked
By dark trees.

12.
Cat on pedestal.
Grey wood.
Puzzle of metal.
Rusted saw.

13.
Choked machine
Nailed to wall.
Bland gaze—
Eyes closing.
He licks his paw.

14.
Cattails in the water
Brown mirror.
Long torso caressing.

15.
Through night's prism
They flash.
Fur quarks—
For a moment
We see them.

BAROQUE VOLUTE

God has no thumb;
But in an intricately
And ornately decorated
Reliquary of porphyry,
Gold, amber and glass
Beneath patterns woven
Of agate, azure and silver
There is a bone
That casts no shadow.
And carved circles whirl
Within circles above—
Where whorls of deep sienna
Crash over rivers of oak
And baroque volutes cascade
Through mahogany currents.
Swirls of wooden torrents
Stream about vast oceans,
Blue skies, white sails,
Saints, gods and seamen.
The glory in gilt
The grand hosannahs
The power's sweeping gesture.
Pink bottomed cherubs
And fat laughing nymphs
Float in great flowering heaven.

BRIDGE OF SIGHS

I.
Not a bride
Sitting at Rialto—
The wedding cake bridge—
They're at home on a bench.

Slavic eyes gelled
Above her impassive mass.
And the ghost
Of that life
Lost
In her flat face.

Harmless satyr,
Heavy-lidded, fondles
That plug of flesh.
And empty hands cupped
Gently tap her breast.

There is no end to the night
On, this, their bridge.
Its up and down
And then to the other side.

While fish from the morning
In markets linger still

Though their guts
Float in the river.

2.
At San Toma
There were silhouettes
In the fiery vault.
Above us the perfect world . . .
But eternal flame
And the shining sword
Kept us on the black water.
The image of glory
We passed shown brightly.
The building lit from below.

3.
Hips pressing stone.
Disturbed reflection.
Yellow shards shifting.
Steps clicking,

Far across the night
Suspended—a kiss blooms
Beyond the white span;
And on black rivers—
The cold structure,
To a face of marble, blue
In pale light, and silent—
Suspened in the darkness.

THE FEAST OF THE REDEEMER

When the plague was over
They sat down to a feast
Of olives, squid and beef

Rags in the grand canal;
Milk and seed in the water.

THE PASSEGGIATA

The debate centered
Around a triangle.
Off the square
That circled
The buttock of Proserpine

Torches flickered in the air.
Long passages like the legs
Of a spider reached
For all directions at once.
And carried through a night of echoes
They found a jewel
Reflecting faint lamps—
A dream on a fancy table.

She reached for what he saw—
A milky light on her arm.
And there was an end to talk.
Beneath the lanterns
Dark in the passage—
Their voices lost on the river.
But caught in the amber glare
Drawn to cold flames
Out from the warm shadow they flew;
It would be a year of ice and trouble
Before they'd consider the long moment's meaning.

St. Peter In Chains

Ants on marzipan.
An angry girl selling cards
False ceilings of dark timber,
The white lights
Poking at Moses.

PO, NOT EDGAR

Oddly familiar
This flattening
These poplar trees
The blue flames—
A child's drawing.
Simple and sure,
Pointing at the sky
The fingers give way—
Near the faint horizon.

Moats but no castles
In Dolo Mirano.
Not a place really
But a direction
Through a somber haze
The grey hills oppressed—
Though oddly familiar.
There are farms but no farmers
In Dolo Mirano.

Not a valley really
But a slow acquiescence
To the water's lapping.
Accepting the dissolution
On which we live.
Not a victory though

But a balance;
And oddly familiar
In a foreign land.

THE KING'S PENIS

A broken column beneath
The cover of dust.
Rome emerging.

A little man with something wrong
Jabbers and motions
But the bus roars on.

I see his arms rise but we turn—
A vision for the end of times.
At the gate of heaven.

Angry saint with a sword
And a man in his underpants—
His legs an unnatural white.

He screams at us—now silent in the sun.
The prophets are darker
Here in the light.

And beside a wall near the tower—
In a golden shadow—
He pulls his pants to the ground.
And bellows.

SENZA TITOLO

The naked poet
Speaks with a man at the station.
His red cow in the rain—
A sad afternoon.

Blue shoes overturned.
Jewel box in the sun
Reflecting the liquid desires obscured.

The tall woman walking,
Her throat cut,
Senses the sure advance of history
Through pink moon-caged alchemy.
Fragmentary passage over bronze
And a white horse pursued
Reaches the dynamic ending.

Woman at the Window in the Deutches Bank

White suit
Cruel face.
Polished pearl.
Hand on hip.
Hard beauty's shell.

I See the City

Open the door
And fly into the light.
I see the city
Shimmering beyond the night.

A thousand pictures
A hundred mirrors
A world of windows,
Perfume, diesel and coffee.

Brocades of plaster
Concrete flowers
The rump of a hero
The dome of God.

BORGO SAN JACOPO

An intricacy of cement.
A puzzle blunt with promise.
A vast curve squared.
A smile of malice.
Long fingers of vacant light
Curl around the corners—
And in those places
Filled with iron and chocolate
They nod—and glance up
And watch us—
Full of detachment.
They yearn not to know
But to bare their souls
And to close their doors
And learn to love us.

AUTOGRILL

Too many numbers
To cross the river
'til an explanation
Was found—the key
Forthcoming.

Astride that road—
Colossus under
A sea of clouds—
In the blue distance
We found the Arno.

THE FORTRESS ORZINI

1

Low skies fall
On grey Sorano.
Underbelly
Dark and bruised
Trolls slowly—
Soiling the sky.
A trail and a smear.
The end is grey Sorano.

2

She stared up at us,
Nose like an eagle,
And denied knowing
That Sorano was falling.

Lips made for an apple.
She said she did not know
Said she never knew
That the town was crumbling—
That it was melting—
That a ravine waited beneath
With jaws wide open—
That it waited for the rest
of grey Sorano.

3
In that field
Near Sorano
We stood looking;
And we smiled.

Though the city leaned
And slid backwards
In to the green unknown
Our thoughts were not there—
But were in the field.
Sunflowers grew tall near Sorano
And uncertain soil held us aloft—
We smiled at the world
That danced around us.

THE VIEW FROM TODI

1

The road, we thought,
Would not end—
Of the Tiber but not on the Tiber.
Garibaldi stands deep
In thoughts of stone.
A door of bricks;
That smooth pull
Of color off
The brush dipped
In the blue and water
Stains a print
Meant for another.

2

In conversation we learn.
Duck, salmon
And small tomatoes
Fresh on a cliff.
The man said
This is his favorite place.
The waiter smiled
As if he understood.
Lentils, lamb, asparagus
And wine.
The cloud over there

That dissipates is purple
And pink and white.

3
The earth below
Is irrational from above
But the green and gold
And brown and yellow
That lie across it
Form a pattern
That we know
From the books
We read about it.

Here the breeze is cool
And the dust has settled
Somewhere else.
Biscuits and wine
Are the subject
Of that man's
Discourse,
And the way to prepare it.

The waiter smiles.
His profile is lost
Above us.
Bread in a basket placed
There on that table
Where the cloth is white, still;
No wine's pink stain
Splashed anywhere on it.

4
The waiter, stone-faced,
Considers the arrangement.
An end is appropriate.
When we rise she ignores us—
As if the world were smaller
Than we ever imagined it
Or than she could explain.
The man smiles
And says they were charming
If only she'd try and see it.

THE COUNT'S UNCLE

Near a wall
Beneath spikes
Of lavender
The count's uncle
Speaks.

Years ago the sun,
Like today,
Settled,
Heat faded
And shadows flooded
The path he walked.

The count's uncle
Speaks:
And holds the vine
To his eye.
Leaves fall to his feet.
He walks to the door
But does not enter.

A breeze, like today,
Blew, those years ago.
The wind died
As he listened.
Today he spoke

Though no one sang.
And in fading light
A scent of lavender
Rose unbidden as it did
Those many years ago.

EEL ON LAGO BORSENA

1

Chasing that car
We could not fathom
That the wrong turns
Were intentional,
And that though the man
Knew what he was doing
He was sadly misinformed.

2

An eel has a spine
But its flesh is delicate
And is good with red wine.
The spider on the menu
Merely calls forth a shudder;
And brushed aside—
We're immersed
Eating bread and butter.

Night Filled with Arrows

The service
Never improved
At Sbarra;
But we left
Well fed.

An emptiness
Engulfed us
And yet we sped
To Onano
Where we did
Not want to be.

The sign said
Pitigliano
But that
Was wrong—
And into a night
Filled with arrows
We fled
Speeding on a road
Well marked
Going nowhere.

DEATH OF THE INNOCENTS

That night
We ate veal.
Dead flies,
Like pepper,
Littered the tile.
Black spots
On a cold map
Of hard red earth.

GELATO

A perfect face appears
Atop Pienza—
Via del Balzello.

Warm wedge of gold;
Pilasters fade
And arches narrow.

There in shadow
Steeped she tastes
Cold lemon gelato.

Piazza San Lorenzo

The leather
Smells like fish.
I fear the sullen look
Of Tuscan women—
And I haven't
The sheen
To catch
Their eyes.

Loosely jointed
Gawky length
Of an English girl—
Having too
Wonderful a time
To notice.

American woman—
Predator
Stalking sights
And never alone.

German girls
Chewing—
Blond, hungry
And too strong
To see me pose.

The nuns—
Well forget the nuns.
The Medici's dead
Across the way—
Lorenzo, wall-eyed and hungry,
Would never
While away the day
Crouched on a step
Beneath an angel
Seeing the world this way.

Fragile Hour

Cup on a ledge
Porcelain flowers.
From the window
Birds beneath me.
Shadows moving.
Fragile hour.

GIRL ON VESPA

Loud sound
Long thigh
Green glass
Red frown
White back
Now gone.

WE ASSUME

The blank earth
Dark matter—
Squired tentatively.
We assume
The light is there.
Fistfuls of dirt
And clots of mud—
The end is nearly
Always
Before us.

MAIN HIGHWAY

1

And now I will speak
Of Nancy's crepes—
Of raspberry preserves,
The lemon curd she served
With scones and of syrup on sausage.

Of a wooden man perched near water's edge
Made from thorns, nails and a chair.
To whom we sang and danced inspired.
That long night was full with us
And glowing we set him afire.

I will speak of ashes in the morning
And thin grey squiggles of wire
Scrawled on the soft debris.
Of strong coffee, remnant smoke
And Jesse laughing.

2

I will speak of stars
On the wall and of the rain
That made us tremble.
The flattened orb of Jupiter sang
While arcs of light embraced us.

Of endless worlds in the crook of his arm
And the mystery of coincidence.
A naked girl who did not float
And the spiraling dance in space.
Of white footprints pregnant with meaning.

And when we drove to that place
Intimations of Kepler's dissonance
Gave us pause; we did not go in
But drove the great curve back home
To find revelation in chocolate tort.

3
I will speak of the magic box
And the tools left by Jesse's father.
Their dark wooden handles smoothed
And oiled by rough hands. His black wand
Held aloft—an incantation to raise the dead.

Japanese plums framed in the window
Were lovely outside with the rest of nature.
My voice rose, loud in enthusiasm—
The spirit freed passed to and fro
And we spoke of things that used to be.

I will speak of short bread and tea
Of spiders hung in ragged banana leaves
Of red rubber boots and porcelain cups
The rising Teche, rich mud and thorny vine
The death of ants and the apotheosis of certain cats.

Index of Poem Titles

Index of Poem First Lines

* 9 7 8 0 9 7 8 5 3 1 1 6 4 *